THE
DUFFER'S
GUIDE TO
RUGBY
Yet Another Try

Gren.

COLUMBUS BOOKS
LONDON

Other books in the Duffer's series:

The Official Duffer's Rules of Golf (John Noble)
The Official Duffer's Rules of Tennis (Bob Adams)
The Duffer's Guide to Golf: A Second Slice (Gren)
The Duffer's Guide to Rugby (Gren)
The Duffer's Guide to Greece (Gren)
The Duffer's Guide to Spain (Gren)
The Duffer's Guide to Coarse Fishing (Mike Gordon)
The Duffer's Guide to Cricket (Gren)

The Duffer's Guide to Snooker (Mike Gordon)
The Duffer's Guide to Booze (Gren)

First published in Great Britain in 1985 by
Columbus Books
Devonshire House, 29 Elmfield Road, Bromley, Kent BR1 1LT

Printed and bound by Clark Constable,
Edinburgh, London, Melbourne

ISBN 0 86287 232 4

CONTENTS

Introduction

Since you have now, dear reader, digested every gem from the first *Duffer's Guide to Rugby,* you will no doubt be thirsting for an even more detailed and sophisticated knowledge of the game you have come to love.

Help is at hand, dear reader. Let our words inspire you to heights of rugby wisdom you would never have dreamt possible.

Types of Rugby Club

Rugby clubs vary considerably and now that you, the duffer, want to join one for reasons of either playing or supporting, it is very important that you select a club into which you will fit. There's nothing worse than finding you've joined a club where the touchline cry is 'I say, chaps, give our steand-orf some protters' when you are more of a 'Big useless fairy! What's the poofter playing at?' type.

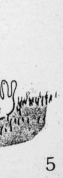

The works side club

There's an air of happy chaos about the works side rugby club. Its members have joined for many reasons, ranging from 'It's good for promotional prospects' to 'That bird I fancy from Accounts is a member'.

The club house is usually an almost derelict shed near the Goods Outwards department while the team play on parks pitches, where if thirteen turn up it's a good week.

Over-enthusiastic duffers beware: join and you'll be captain or club chairman in a week.

The traditional club

This kind of club lives in the past and hopes one day to regain its former glory. The current players know they are only representing players of the 'great years' when the club boasted fourteen internationals in its first XV.

The walls are covered with faded prints of the teams of yesteryear while players of today are lucky to be recognized as they try to get past a grumpy, blazered and tied ex-trialist for a drink in the members' bar.

Duffers should only join such a club if rejected by all others.

The old boys' club

This club is usually a sort of an apprentice snob club where all sorts of after-match drinking games take place. It also features wild and bawdy songs sung by people who, during their sober rest-of-the-week existence, would protest about people who behave like themselves.

The players tend to be faded stars or never-quite-made-it-would-have-beens who are never quite sure when they're past it.

The duffer will enjoy this type of club and should push his way in through the doctors, dentists, solicitors and accountants who hog the bar.

The village rugby club

A very nice type of club, where they don't usually take the Saturday fixture too seriously. It's more of a social centre than a real rugby club and half the committee wouldn't recognize a loop move if they saw one — which is unlikely as their side could never produce one.

The players in such a club usually consist of ex-school players, a sprinkling of ex-university, and one or two defrocked soccer players.

The duffer will always enjoy the village club.

OLD RUSTIC
RFC 1836

Types of Playing Area

There are almost as many types of playing surface as there are ticket scroungers on International day.

Some players feign injury after they've inspected the pitch for an away venue, while others sarcastically ask the home coach what studs he'd recommend for asphalt and glass.

The assault course

This type of pitch varies from bog-like at the club end to hard rocky outcrops at the other. In between, you'll find several crevices and the odd unexploded bomb sticking out here and there, which all go to make the games interesting.

The golden rule on such grounds is to get rid of the ball as soon as you get it and under no circumstances to run with it as you never know what maiming tackler lurks round the next boulder.

11

HOW D'YOU WANT IT, LADS — UP HILL OR DOWNHILL FIRST HALF?

The Welsh valley ground

These grounds don't boast flags in the usual places. Instead, they have road signs saying 'Beware 1 in 4 gradient' or 'Beware falling rocks'.

It's difficult, too, for the visiting wingman, who looks like a world-class even-timer playing downhill in the first half but is reduced to a jelly-kneed breathless mess by halfway through the second. Visiting teams should also beware the strolling sheep on such grounds. Many a hamstring has gone trying to side-step a marauding baa-baa.

This type of ground has one distinct advantage over most other types — it never gets flooded.

12

The parks ground

There are normally so many pitches on parks grounds that the golden rule is never to go off to retrieve a ball that's been booted out of play – you'll have to collect it from another nearby pitch. And as your shirt isn't the colour of either side playing there, both teams will thump you. Then, when you finally stagger back with the ball, you won't be able to find the pitch you started out from.

Duffers should always aim to play on parks grounds – it's easy to creep away when you've had enough.

YOU ARE HERE

13

The 'last-year-it-was-under-water' reclaimed bog

You can always tell when a club uses this type of pitch. Little tell-tale signs like the tide timetables are printed on the club's letter-heading and the touch judges turn up in waders. The trainer, if called upon, is accompanied by a couple of chaps from the RNLI.

The manicured lawn

The sight of this lush green sward with its gleaming white pitch markings inhibits most visiting players, who are already twelve points down before they are certain they've not strayed on to the bowling green by mistake.

Visiting Welsh teams, too, are always put off, and it takes them until half-time to get used to playing on a flat pitch.

The most annoying thing about such a ground is that every time there's a stoppage in play, the groundsman comes on to replace divots and swear at the players responsible.

PLEASE KEEP OFF THE GRASS

How to Play Dirty

There are many ways to play dirty. The experienced player will use any method at his command without resorting to actual violence — the principle being to shake the confidence of your opponent and let his imagination ruin his game.

The real duffer should try only one of these per game until he becomes reasonably proficient, whereupon he should use them as often as possible. (Remember the adage 'All's fair in love, war and rugby'.)

The SAS ploy

Look deeply into the eyes of your opposite number and make your right eye twitch as you say, 'I never thought any club would let me play again after that business which led to their kicking me out of the SAS team for being over-vigorous.'

He won't come near you all afternoon.

The martial arts ploy

In the first line-out say to their psychopath, 'I think I should warn you, my hands are registered with the county police as dangerous weapons.'

The dirty weekend ploy

As you crush your head against the others' in the first scrummage, whisper in their hooker's ear, 'I know a bloke who spent the weekend at your house while you were away on the last Easter tour.'

This is guaranteed to upset his concentration for the rest of the afternoon.

The frog ploy

When their star scrummager is pinned into a ruck, take advantage by shoving a frog up his shirt or down his shorts – he won't go into a scrummage for the rest of the afternoon.

20

The bootlace ploy

When you see a pair of opposition boots sticking out of the scrummage, tie the laces together – it really upsets some players.

The pal-of-the-ref ploy

You've never met the ref before, but still you say to him in a loud voice, 'Don't forget, ref, I don't expect any favours from you just because I saved your life in that boating accident.'

From then on, every decision in favour of your team will get the opposition jumpily frustrated. You will then, of course, capitalize on their jittery mistakes.

Training and How to Avoid It

Training is, of course, unnecessary, as any decent player will tell you. But you, the duffer, can't be expected to know all the little schemes devised to avoid it that have been tried and tested over the years. So read on, dear duffer, select and use tactfully the excuse that suits you best.

Pay off the coach

This, though somewhat lacking in subtlety, is very effective, as no coach (any experienced player will confirm this) could resist the sight of a fiver being proffered by your tiny little hand while you say something like: 'Look coach, say no more – my wife wants me home early tonight' (wink, wink); 'Wedding anniversary celebration, y'know what I mean?'

His fat, grubby hand will instantly envelop the fiver, enabling you to nip back to the club bar where, pint in hand, you can watch old international matches on the big-screen video.

24

Afraid you'll peak too soon

This ploy requires a little acting ability, so it should only be tried by double-glazing salesmen, Jehovah's Witnesses or local politicians.

Ever concerned about the team's performance, you quietly suggest to the coach that his progressive ideas on the game have brought you to peak just a few days too soon — and if he insists on your training tonight, it's his fault not yours if you are stale by match day. 'It's up to you, of course, coach,' you say.

It always works. All coaches are sensitive to blame.

The bandaged-foot routine

This one never fails — you make a hinged plaster of paris cast which can be bandaged shut over your perfectly good leg.

When you report on crutches on training night, you beg to be allowed on. Your horrified coach stops you as you plead, with tears in your eyes: 'The doc only had it plastered as a precaution. It's not broken, I'm sure.'

How could he then drop you from the side when you turn up, miraculously cured, on match-day crying, 'Huh, doctors! What do they know?'?

The floodlight allergy

This has to be used with caution, and only when the training session is held under floodlights.

You explain to your harassed coach that, if he's sure the club's insurance policy covers your particular problem, you're happy to train, but the floodlights make you come out in an irritating and highly contagious rash which sometimes leaves men impotent. You support the story with some details about it have something to do with your mother having a tragic affair with an Electricity Board fitter before you were born.

It works every time. Coaches are dead scared of impotence.

27

Midweek training makes you too tired

You can use this only if (a) you are a very valuable member of the side and (b) the coach hasn't already had a bet on the opposition for Saturday's game.

You simply say, 'Sorry, coach, I've wrestled with this problem. I don't know how to put it, but if I train mid-week I'm too tired to play on Saturday. The decision is yours. I'll do whatever you want.'

Coaches are afraid of decisions so it'll be left to you – and you'll go back to the club bar with the guy who's afraid he'll peak too soon and the one who's paid off the coach.

I Play Rugby Because . . .

There are many reasons for picking on rugby as the game that claims your enthusiasm — reasons which would probably surprise the sensitive duffer.

I like thumping people.

I enjoy being in the showers with hairy men.

I find hooped jerseys so much more flattering than stripes.

I like swearing in public.

My VAT man is my outside half – I enjoy giving him hospital passes.

I don't enjoy the game at all – but I like getting drunk afterwards.

I hope one day to be interviewed by Nigel Starmer-Smith.

I'll do anything to get away from the wife.

Twice a season I get a chance to play against the bloke my wife ran off with.

Touchline posing – it's a great way of chatting up the birds.

How to Become Club Captain

Believe it or not, there are some players who *want* to be club captain (most captains get elected, as you probably know, because they are the only playing members not at the meeting when the captaincy becomes vacant).

For the sake of all those headstrong, egotistical duffers who see team captaincy as an achievement, here are some of the more traditional methods of getting it (apart from the aforementioned failure to turn up at captain-selection meetings).

Get Daddy to buy the club

There are two drawbacks to this ploy: (a) Daddy has to be very rich and (b) if he is rich, why are you playing rugby instead of spending the winter sailing round the Greek islands?

The system is simple: if they won't let you be captain after several tantrums and a pouting fit, you get Daddy to buy the club lock, stock and barrel (particularly the barrel). This being done, you appoint yourself captain supreme and pick only your little friends. This may not result in a successful team but, boy, will the opposition enjoy playing against you!

DADDY DAHLING, RODDERS WANTS TO ASK YOU FOR MY HAND.

Threaten to marry the president's daughter

This one works only if you, the duffer, are God's gift to the ladies. You then, with all the charm you can muster, sweep the president's daughter off her feet. She becomes totally besotted by you, while you present yourself to her father as a drunken, foul-mouthed, no-prospect bully. When he hears that you and his darling daughter wish to marry, he'll be so horrified that he'll try to buy you off. Your price: the club captaincy.

As a variation, you can use the same ploy substituting the president's lovely wife for his daughter.

Creep around the committee

The committee, as opposed to the players, do care about the choice of club captain. They like to think that the club is represented by a sober person who can think deeply about the game while also being delighted to make speeches at the drop of a headband.

You therefore play up to this by walking round the club sipping Malvern water and muttering about the tactics of support running while simultaneously writing a speech. This will bring you to the committee's attention either as a potential captain or a raving lunatic. Either way, you'll probably get the job.

Pretend you're a natural leader

For this you must force yourself to sit on every committee within the club. At meetings, take every opportunity to speak up loudly and long on behalf of someone else, that is, the players, the supporters, the stewards – anyone other than yourself. Soon you will acquire the reputation of being not a glory-seeking manipulator, but a fearless martyr.

Could anyone else have those qualities and not be asked to captain the club? Congratulations – you've got the job.

Creep around the players

This isn't really necessary as they are very happy for anyone to be captain as long as it isn't them. But they won't tell you this, of course – not as long as you sycophantically continue buying them drinks to gain their favour.

FIFTEEN PINTS OF BITTER – TWELVE LAGERS – TWO GINS AND TONICS...

Never Believe an Ex-player

As a newcomer to the rugby scene, you will probably believe all the tales of great feats told at the bar by ex-players. You must remember that ex-players have one thing in common: their recall of certain incidents has been adjusted to add to the dramatic effect of the story – or to boost the teller's ego. In short, all ex-players are liars, so beware.

1. *'I side-stepped two players, then handed off another three or four as I swerved round them before sprinting fifty yards for the line . . .'*

This really means: 'Somebody pushed me and the ball over the line from a yard out.'

2. 'I realized the crosswind was strong so I decided to place the ball rather than kick it out of my hands. I placed it carefully and, allowing for the wind, struck the ball sweetly between the posts.'

This really means: 'I was trying for a long touch-finder.'

IT'S A WELL-KNOWN FACT THAT THE SELECTORS AND THAT OUTSIDE HALF'S MOTHER HAD A LITTLE UNDERSTANDING...

3. 'Of course, it wasn't surprising I didn't get a cap after what I told them. Call themselves selectors? I told them a few home truths. I wouldn't trust you lot to pick our kid's school side, I said . . .'

This really means: 'I didn't get a cap because I was rubbish.'

4. *'I was with them for eight seasons and when I left the club it just went to pieces.'*

This really means: 'It's not surprising, really, that the club went down the drain. I took most of the bar stock and had all the club's money transferred to my private account.'

SORRY, NOT TONIGHT, GIRLS – BIG GAME TOMORROW.

5. *'What an Easter tour! Hundreds of raving birds throwing themselves at us . . .'*

This really means: 'Two girls at a bus-stop waved at our coach.'

6. 'I knew he was a good 'un. Ex-All Black, all muscle and bone — nasty with it — so I had to make my first tackle tell. When he came rampaging through, I was waiting for him. Bang! I hit him. That was the last I saw of him that afternoon.'

This really means: 'I didn't regain consciousness until after their team coach had gone.'

7. 'Of course, I had my share of offers to go and play Rugby League.'

What he failed to add was: '. . . mainly from my own teammates.'

8. 'We were losing six-nil with five minutes to go. Our captain didn't have a clue – so someone had to take charge. This is what we do, I said – and within a minute we'd put twelve points on the board.'

What he forgot to mention was that the opposition added another eighteen.

9. *'So I told them — either the selection committee goes or I do.'*

What he didn't say was, 'So I went'.

yes

How to Attract the Attention of the Selectors

Now that you are developing from a duffer to a novice player, it's quite understandable that you should wish to become selected for a representative side.

This has nothing to do with talent for the game — a quick look at the current district, county or national squad will soon confirm this. No, it has everything to do with attracting the selectors' bored gaze away from the actual game (probably the eighth they've seen this week) to notice something new. This in itself will provide a form of relief, and if you are the player responsible there's a chance it will be your name they remember when the other, better performers are faded memories.

Bleed a lot

There's nothing selectors like more than to see a player regain consciousness (in this case after feigning unconsciousness) with blood pouring from an obvious massive gash above the hairline (thinned tomato sauce), refusing all efforts to make him pack it in (*à la* Rives) and manfully pitching back into the fray — leading by example and all that sort of thing.

Use this ploy two or three times each half and you're in the next representative XV — it always works.

HONESTLY, CHAPS — MERELY A SEVERED ARTERY — LET'S GET ON WITH THE GAME

Dye your hair blonde

The English selectors are suckers for this little ploy. They love longish, flaxen-haired backs. We've seen players in the English XV who were actually picked while sitting next to the Chairman of Selectors in a his 'n' hers hair salon.

The dodge is simple. Grow your hair shoulder-length, slosh the dye on and run around a lot, especially on the same side of the field as the selectors (some have a little difficulty with their sight). Don't worry about the ball, but run about. Properly done, we'll guarantee you'll be in the squad before you're halfway through your first bottle of dye.

Be a peace-maker

Selectors like seeing fearless players leaping in to stop fights without a thought for themselves. Selectors (being basically simple-minded) see this as an indication of the qualities of leadership and fair play, and they'll think you can probably make after-dinner speeches as well.

So off you go stopping fights, stopping snarling sessions, stopping, in fact, anything remotely like physical confrontation. After all, the selectors won't know that you actually started the aggro, will they?

If you leap in to save the ref a bashing, you'll be in the next representative side whether you want to or not!

DESIST! MIGHT IS NOT RIGHT.

Make sure they know who you are

This necessitates you bribing someone on the public address system to use your name whenever possible.

Whoever scores your side's points the spectators (and, therefore, selectors) will be told it's you. Claim credit for tries, kicks, drop goals and carrying off injured players and make sure you're mentioned at half time for donating the ball.

When the selectors compliment you in the players' bar afterwards, say casually, 'Thanks. I hope I'll be back to match fitness soon', as you gently press your name-emblazoned photograph into each selectorial palm.

Wear a college scarf

Selectors are suckers for this one. Find out if one of the selectors ever went to a college (or if any ever went to a school) and wear the old student's scarf.

There's nothing more strongly guaranteed to bring you to the attention of a selector than the sight of someone running on in his old college scarf. You will be pointed out to the other selectors and he'll tell them what a good player you are. They, upon seeing this mark of superior education flapping around your neck as you run up and down the touchline, will make a mental note to select you as soon as possible. Selectors like picking intelligent players. They're less trouble in the after-match booze-ups.

How to Bluff Your Way Through Clubhouse Chat

It's only natural that you, the duffer, being new to the rugby scene, should feel out of things when it comes to idle conversation that takes place at the club bar. Don't be embarrassed about your lack of knowledge. Armed with just a few intelligent lines ready to be tossed in whenever the conversation lulls, you will soon be hailed as one of the club's great thinkers about the game. It doesn't matter if they don't make sense – no one really listens, anyway. But beware – don't overdo it. You don't want to become club chairman already, do you?

Their scrum half was weak on passing right — we should have capitalized on it.

Couldn't we see how slow their outside half was when he had to come off his left foot?

Their flankers didn't compensate each other.

Frankly, I'd have played an outside half who reads the options and is much more committed to an all-round game.

Why didn't he go left when their defence was committed?

It was obvious that their left side was exposed to direct running with support.

He called '19-23-26' when it was obvious from the stand that this line-out needed a 19-11-10.

They should have held on a fraction longer to release our overlap player.

Do you remember Van der Pugh used that to great effect during the '74 tour?

Impressive Things to Shout from the Touchline

Now that you know about bluffing while standing pint-in-hand at the club bar, it's only natural that you will want to continue this impressive array of rugby thoughts from the touchline.

This, too, is easy once you have mastered a few well-phrased observations.

You can get him here – put the ball high into the sun.

Watch the alignment, backs.

No, no, no, full back. We needed to counter-attack then.

Remember their weakness from last season, boys? – Exploit it now!

Watch the encroachment, boys.

What's the matter, ref – doesn't law seven apply any more?

There's a double reverse blindside move on here, boys.

Watch the binding this side, ref.

He's doing it *again*, ref!

Where were you then, back row?

How to Look Like a Great Player

There is nothing worse for making you look like a rank beginner (or even a useless pratt) than to take the field in the basic standard kit as used by your chosen club.

To give the impression that you are a good player you must exude an air of experienced ability. In order to achieve this there are certain additions and alterations that you must make to your playing strip before you have the inner confidence to adopt the sort of swagger that belies your playing ability.

The shirt

Always doctor your shirt as soon as it is given to you. Cut through the stitching at the collar and where the sleeves meet the shoulders so that at the slightest touch they will part – leaving the wearer looking as if he's been in the thick of things all afternoon.

Tearing the club badge half off is a nice touch too, as this lends an air of rebellious swashbuckling aggression, worth at least six points to your side.

The shorts

Some cheapskate clubs are quite happy to kit out their players with the less expensive soccer shorts – the ones without pockets and waist ties. Never, ever wear these: you'll look like a fairy reject from a training film, and your career could come to a very untimely end.

You must always, when not actually involved in the game, thrust your hands deeply into the pockets of these shorts. It looks as though you are calm, in control and thinking tactics – which impresses those opposition yobs wearing soccer shorts.

Your shorts must never, ever be of exactly the same colour as those of the rest of your team. They must be either bleach-faded blue or dirty white. This gives the impression you've been around a bit.

The socks

Your socks should never, ever match your club jersey. Instead they should be impressive socks (available from the Impressive Sock Shop, Twickenham), so colourful that your opposite number is hypnotized by them. He spends most of the game expecting you to do something spectacular because your impressive socks have hinted to him that you are a secret guest player – probably a de-frocked All Black on the Harlequins' books. By the time he realizes that you're an even worse player than he is it'll be too late. Your side will have almost won.

JUST GIMME THE BALL AND POINT ME TOWARDS THE LINE.

Bandages

You must wear the bandages with subtlety. If you are a forward go for the head bandage — always, of course, milky white when you take the field. When you rise from the first scrummage with it oozing blood (from a carefully-secreted tomato sauce sachet) and glare about, you will be feared for the rest of the game.

Backs should wear the knee bandage or thigh strapping (favoured by full backs). Both give the impression that you've played a bit, and of someone too tough to allow such trivialities as torn muscles, hamstrings, tendons or a knee cap dropping off to stop you getting at the opposition.

Gumshields

Unfortunately, the now-common practice of wearing gumshields has partly put a stop to the old ploy of painting a few front teeth out so that you can bestow a menacing smile on your opposite number.

However, this can be overcome reasonably effectively by painting teeth on to your gumshields, then painting a few out again – you'll terrorize outside halfs forever.

Boots

Boots are dead giveaways in the sort of rugby that the wearer is able to play, so remember the importance of preparing your boots well before you take the field.

There are three basic types of boots with which you can influence your opponents.

1. The speed-merchant models

All you need to do is to tart up the boots, even if they are brand-new. Iron the day-glo laces, highly polish the fading toe caps and when they are on you (with your hands thrust deeply into the aforementioned pockets) run on the spot, click-clicking on the concrete outside the opposition's dressing-rooms. This gives you an air of confidence and your opponents the idea that you're a speed merchant – and your being deceptively slow on the pitch will fool them again.

2. *The I've-seen-it-all-before models*

These are a favourite with slow forwards. You have to give your boots the look of being old campaigners. Even if they are new, scag them up a bit – bleach the toe caps, throw out the poncy day-glo yellow laces, replace them with garden twine or even old, faded, knotted laces. Once you have them on, use very wide elastic tape to stick them to your ankle – the macho effect is quite inspirational.

The final horrifying touch is to arrange the good old tomato sauce sachet under the lace holes through which the sachet can be pierced – at a time to suit yourself – for maximum bloody effect.

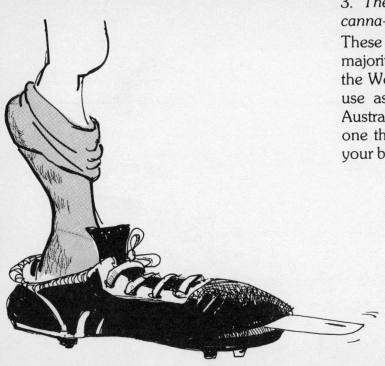

3. *The I'm-gonna-make-you-an-offer-you-canna-refuse models*

These models are not really acceptable in the majority of clubs — though there are one or two in the Welsh valleys who turn a blind eye to their use as there are clubs in New Zealand and Australia that positively encourage them. But one thing is for sure: while wearing this model your burst for the line isn't going to be impeded.